Read and Play
Trains

by Jim Pipe

Aladdin/Watts
London • Sydney

train

2

Here is a **train**.

A **train** pulls a big load.

3

engine

4

A train has a strong **engine**.

driver

A train has a **driver**.

5

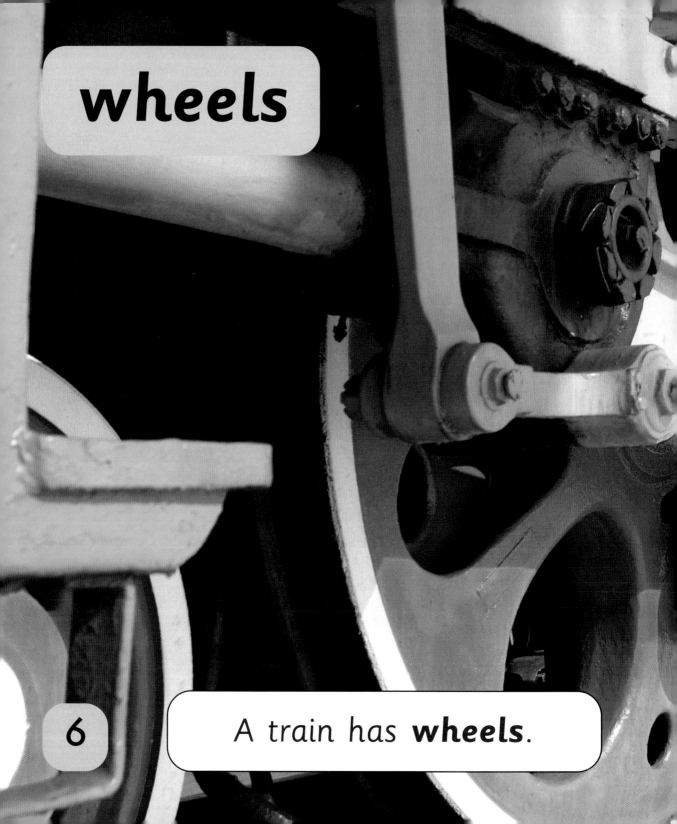

wheels

6

A train has **wheels**.

Wheels roll around.

7

tracks

8

A train runs on **tracks**.

A **track** has two rails.

9

station

お弁当

10

A train stops at a **station**.

People get on. All aboard!

11

wagons

This train pulls **wagons**.

passengers

This train carries **passengers**. 13

express

An **express** train is fast.

hill

A **hill** train is slow.

15

steam

16

This is a **steam** train.

It has a **steam** engine.

17

over

This train goes **over** the ground.

18

under

This train goes **under** the ground.

19

What am I?

passengers

driver

wheels

tracks

20

Match the words and pictures.

How many?

Can you count the trains?

21

What noise?

Clickety clack!

Chuff! Chuff!

Whoosh!

Screech!

Make a sound like a train!

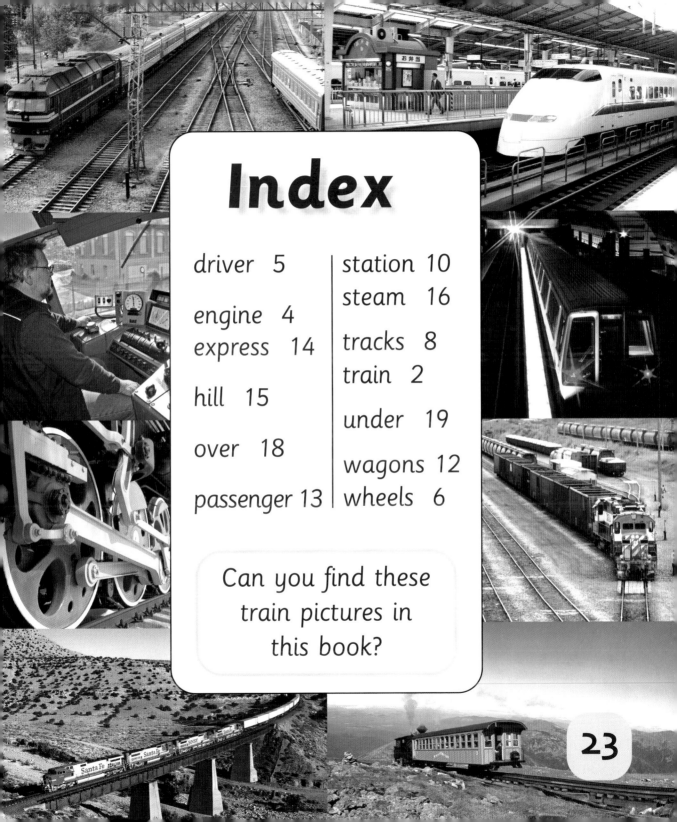

Index

Can you find these
train pictures in
this book?

For Parents and Teachers

Questions you could ask:

p.2 What can you see in this picture? Point out the four locomotives at front and line of wagons behind.

p. 4 Why does a train need a strong engine? To pull a heavy load. A locomotive weighs about the same as 50 cars. Some trains are over 7 km long!

p. 5 Would you like to drive a train? Encourage role play: drivers need to know which route they are taking, to follow signals, to stop the train so passengers can get on board, and blow the whistle!

p. 8 How does a train go left or right? You can't steer a train like a car because it runs on tracks. Look at the wheels on page 7. Special switches called points help trains to change tracks.

p. 13 Where can you go on a train? Unlike a car, trains can only travel on tracks. Trains connect big cities as well as smaller towns. On very long journeys passengers sleep on board the train.

p. 15 Why do you think a hill train is slow? Because it has to go up a hill. Most trains travel on the flat.

When they come to a hill, they go through a tunnel.

p. 16 How can you spot a steam train? Look for the big white clouds of steam coming from the engine and listen for the "chuff chuff" sound.

p. 20 Who am I? If they need a clue, children can look back to pages 5, 6, 8 and 13.

Activities you could do:

• Ask the reader to draw a simple train, writing labels for engine, wheels, wagons, tracks etc.

• Line up chairs to create a train. Put numbers on the chairs and hand out tickets. You can use props such as suitcases, maps, cap, whistles etc.

• Ask the reader to describe a train journey they might like to go on, e.g. steam train.

• Introduce trains by reading aloud stories such as *Thomas the Tank Engine*, *Ivor the Engine* or *The Little Engine That Could*.

• Show children how to make train whistle sounds by blowing across the top of a plastic bottle.

© Aladdin Books Ltd 2007

Designed and produced by
Aladdin Books Ltd
2/3 Fitzroy Mews
London W1T 6DF

First published in 2007
in Great Britain
by Franklin Watts
338 Euston Road
London NW1 3BH

Franklin Watts Australia
Level 17/207 Kent Street
Sydney NSW 2000

Franklin Watts is a division of Hachette Children's Books.

ISBN 978 0 7496 7505 9

A catalogue record for this book is available from the British Library.

Dewey Classification: 385
Printed in Malaysia
All rights reserved

Series consultant
Zoe Stillwell is an Early Years teacher at Pewley Down Infant School, Guildford.

Photocredits:
l-left, r-right, b-bottom, t-top, c-centre, m-middle
All photos from istockphoto.com except: 1, 14, 21, 22, tl & tr — ALSTOM transport. 2-3, 19, 23mtr & bl — Corbis. 5, 20tl, 23mtl— Andreas Neumann. 18 — Flat Earth.